Searchlight BOOKS™

Animal
Superpowers

Walking
Sticks

and Other Amazing
Camouflage

Laura Hamilton Waxman

Lerner Publications ◆ Minneapolis

In memory of Sumah

Lerner Publications Company
A division of Lerner Publishing Group, Inc.
241 First Avenue North
Minneapolis, MN 55401 USA

For reading levels and more information, look up this title at www.lernerbooks.com.

Library of Congress Cataloging-in-Publication Data

Names: Waxman, Laura Hamilton.
Title: Walking sticks and other amazing camouflage / Laura Hamilton Waxman.
Description: Minneapolis : Lerner Publications, [2017] | Series: Searchlight books. Animal superpowers | Audience: Age 8–11. | Audience: Grade 4 to 6. | Includes bibliographical references and index.
Identifiers: LCCN 2016018157 (print) | LCCN 2016018522 (ebook) | ISBN 9781512425499 (lb : alk. paper) | ISBN 9781512431179 (pb : alk. paper) | ISBN 9781512428247 (eb pdf)
Subjects: LCSH: Camouflage (Biology)—Juvenile literature. | Animals—Color—Juvenile literature. | Stick insects—Juvenile literature.
Classification: LCC QL767 .W39 2017 (print) | LCC QL767 (ebook) | DDC 591.47/2—dc23

LC record available at https://lccn.loc.gov/2016018157

Manufactured in the United States of America
1-41317-23261-5/27/2016

Contents

Chapter 1

WALKING STICKS

Animals in the wild spend their lives hiding and seeking. But for them, it's not a game. It's a matter of survival. An animal that stands out draws attention to itself. If it's prey, it might be more likely to become a meal. If it's a predator, it will have a harder time catching enough to eat. So how do animals hide? Many of them use camouflage.

The natural world is a dangerous place for most animals. What's one way they survive?

Camouflage helps an animal blend in or fool other animals. The walking stick does both of these things extremely well. This insect lives in wooded places and tropical forests. It gets its name from its unusual appearance. The bug looks like a brown or green stick with long, twig-like legs.

The smallest walking stick could fit on your thumb. The largest is a little bit longer than a ruler.

Walking sticks make a filling meal for many predators. That's why birds, reptiles, spiders, and mammals hunt for them. But walking sticks can't get away from these predators easily. Walking sticks aren't fast runners. So they can't race from danger. They aren't good fliers either. Some walking sticks have such small wings that they can't fly at all. Others don't even have wings! That's why their camouflage is so important.

IF A WALKING STICK DOESN'T
BLEND IN, IT COULD BECOME LUNCH!

Fitting Right In

During the day, a walking stick often hides in the leaves of a tree. Most of the time, it barely moves. By staying still, the walking stick blends in with the tree. Predators think the insect is a stick, not food. They pass right by the walking stick.

Walking sticks are active at night, when the darkness hides them.

When a walking stick does move, it still uses camouflage. It walks slowly down a branch on its long,

skinny legs. And as it walks, it gently sways back and forth. To other animals, it looks like a twig blowing in the breeze. This trick helps protect it from predators.

A passing bird might think this walking stick is part of the tree.

Winging It

Some walking sticks use their wings to escape from predators. Underneath the wings are bright patches of color. If a predator comes too close, the insect snaps open its wings. The predator is attracted by the flash of color and zooms toward it. But by then, the insect has folded its wings and dropped to the ground. It looks like an ordinary stick again and is safely hidden.

The wings of walking sticks are invisible when they're folded shut.

Compare It!

The leaf-tailed gecko is a lot like the walking stick. This lizard hides by looking like part of the tree. It's the same color and texture as a twisting, rotting leaf. Like a walking stick, a leaf-tailed gecko stays very still in the forest. It also uses color to deal with predators that spot it. This lizard has a bright red mouth. When a predator comes near, the lizard opens its jaws wide. Many predators are frightened by its big, red mouth. They stay away.

A leaf-tailed gecko is often brown, and its skin is covered with thin lines. The lines look like veins on a leaf.

Camouflaged Eggs

Camouflage helps walking sticks before they're even born! That's because many walking stick eggs look like seeds. This disguises them from the larvas that feed on insect eggs. Many female walking sticks lay their eggs on the ground. But they often don't lay their eggs all at once. They lay just one each day. That way, the eggs look like tiny seeds scattered on the forest floor.

Some walking sticks protect their eggs by hiding them in places that predators can't reach.

Chapter 2

PYGMY SEA HORSES

A predator has to look extra hard to spot a pygmy sea horse. This sea creature uses camouflage to blend in with its surroundings. Like all sea horses, pygmy sea horses are a kind of fish. They are called sea horses because their curved heads look like horses' heads. Of all the sea horses, the pygmy sea horse is one of the best at hiding.

A pygmy sea horse is named for its size. What does the word *pygmy* mean?

12

Pygmy means "something very small." A pygmy
sea horse is about the size of a small paper clip. That
makes it one of the tiniest sea horses in the ocean.
Some pygmy sea horses are yellow with orange bumps.
Others are purple with pink bumps.

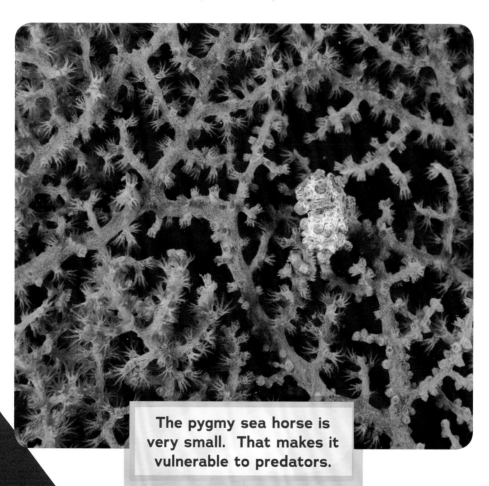

**The pygmy sea horse is
very small. That makes it
vulnerable to predators.**

Clinging for Life

A pygmy sea horse swims very slowly. It can't zoom away from fish, crabs, or other predators. In fact, it doesn't move much at all. It spends most of its life clinging to coral with its tail. That way, it won't accidentally float into a predator's mouth!

PYGMY SEA HORSES NEED TO HOLD ON TIGHT!

Compare It!

Can you spot the animal on this tree trunk? It's a gray tree frog. It's another animal that can be hard to find. Like the sea horse, it's a clingy creature. This amphibian uses its sticky toe pads to cling to trees. Its bumpy, patterned skin matches tree bark. The tree frog can also make its skin darker or lighter. Its color changes depending on the temperature, season, and time of day.

The gray tree frog lives in woods and forests.

Pygmy sea horses hide in a type of coral called a sea fan. The sea horse matches the color of the sea fan perfectly. Even its bumps match the shape and color of the coral's bumps. These features make the sea horse nearly impossible to find.

Just like pygmy sea horses, many sea fans are orange or purple.

A Sea Horse's Camouflage Is Born

For most kinds of animals, the females give birth to their young. But pygmy sea horses are different. The male usually carries sea horse eggs in a pouch. The baby pygmies hatch in the pouch and then enter the water.

These babies aren't born brightly colored like coral. They're a dull brown. They don't have round bumps on them either. But that changes once they choose their coral home. Slowly, their body color begins to match the color of the coral. They grow bumps to match the coral too!

Pygmy sea horses are so well camouflaged that scientists didn't know about them until recently. They only discovered the animals while studying sea fans in a lab.

Chapter 3

PTARMIGANS

Ptarmigans are tough birds that can survive long, deadly winters. They spend most of their lives on the tundra or high in the mountains. But harsh conditions aren't the only danger these animals face. Skillful hunters, such as golden eagles and red foxes, prey on ptarmigans. Ptarmigans use camouflage to avoid becoming a predator's next meal.

A ptarmigan's camouflage doesn't stay the same all year. When does it change?

Changing with the Seasons

In winter, a ptarmigan's habitat is covered with snow. In spring and summer, the melting snow exposes a brown, rocky environment. How can the ptarmigan blend into such different surroundings? Its camouflage changes with the seasons.

The state bird of Alaska is a type of ptarmigan called the willow ptarmigan. It fits right into the landscape of Alaska's snowy winters and warmer springs.

In winter, a ptarmigan's feathers are pure white. It even has white feathers on its legs and on the tops and bottoms of its feet. The feathers help the bird blend in. They also protect it from the cold and snow. Stiff feathers under each foot turn the bird's feet into a kind of snowshoe. The feathers keep the bird from sinking into the snow as it walks.

IN WINTER, PTARMIGANS LIVE TOGETHER IN LARGE GROUPS.

In spring, the ptarmigan grows new feathers. These feathers are often a mix of white with brown or gray. This coloring helps the ptarmigan hide from predators. A ptarmigan spends most of its time on the ground. Its spring and summer coloring helps it blend in with rocks, shadows, and plants.

Three types of ptarmigans live in North America. Each type has a slightly different spring coloring.

Compare It!

The arctic fox is another animal that lives in the tundra. Like the ptarmigan, its coloring changes each spring. In winter, an arctic fox's warm fur is pure white. It even has fur on the bottoms of its paws to help it walk over snow. In spring, the fox's fur is dark brown or gray. Its light and dark camouflage helps it stay hidden from small lemmings and the other prey it stalks.

The arctic fox's color change helps it hunt more easily.

Timing It Right

Some types of male ptarmigans keep their white feathers for a longer time than the females do. That's likely because spring is mating season. Staying white helps the males stand out. They can more easily attract the attention of female ptarmigans.

After mating, the female lays her eggs in a shallow nest on the ground. She has already changed color. Her dark feathers help her blend in with the habitat and keep her eggs safe.

Camouflage protects this mother and her eggs.

Chapter 4

MIMIC OCTOPUSES

A shark glides through the ocean in search of prey. Out of the corner of its eye, it sees a lionfish. The shark swims away from its enemy. It doesn't know that it has been fooled. What it actually saw was a mimic octopus.

Mimic octopuses can change to look like different animals. Why do they do this?

Mimic octopuses don't have many ways to fight off predators. They don't have sharp teeth or claws. They don't make poison or use stingers. Instead, mimic octopuses are masters of disguise. They are also masters of the quick change. They can change their coloring, shape, and even skin texture. They use this type of camouflage to scare or confuse predators.

These octopuses are skillful copycats. Scientists only discovered their true identity about twenty years ago.

Shape-Shifting

Most mimic octopuses live in the Pacific Ocean near the nation of Indonesia. They change their appearance to look like other animals in their habitat. Some of these animals are deadly. Others cause pain or have a bad taste. All of them are unpleasant to predators.

Mimic octopuses may be able to look like at least fifteen different animals.

Sea snakes are some of the most poisonous snakes on the planet.

One animal the octopus can look like is the poisonous sea snake. The mimic octopus changes its brown-and-white stripes to yellow-and-black ones. It pulls six of its arms into its body and stretches its other two arms in opposite directions. Then it waves them like slithering snakes. This fools nearby predators and keeps them away.

Compare It!

Like the mimic octopus, the goldenrod crab spider can change how it looks. But it changes to hide from prey rather than to scare away predators. The crab spider seeks out yellow or white flowers. Then it makes its body yellow or white to match. The flowers attract bees, butterflies, and other insects. When an insect comes along, the spider grabs it and shoots it with venom.

This spider is waiting until something good comes along to eat.

A mimic octopus can also change to look like a toxic sole fish. The octopus folds all of its arms close to its body. It makes itself flat and leaf-shaped. Then the octopus ripples in the water. Its shape and rippling movement look a lot like the sole fish.

THIS OCTOPUS CHANGES ITS
SHAPE AND THE WAY IT SWIMS!

The jellyfish is another disguise for the mimic octopus. First, the octopus puffs up its head. Meanwhile, it lets its long arms gently float above it. Then it slowly rises and sinks in the ocean the way a jellyfish does.

This octopus can even look like a rock. To do that, it changes both the color and texture of its skin.

Jellyfish can sting other animals that get too close.

Making Choices

How do mimic octopuses choose which animal or object to change into? Scientists believe it depends on the predator. For example, one of the mimic octopus's predators is the damselfish. When this fish comes near, the octopus will turn into a sea snake. Sea snakes hunt and eat damselfish.

The mimic octopus makes itself look like the animal that will be scariest to a predator.

Chapter 5

LEOPARDS

A leopard tracks a graceful gazelle with its sharp eyes. This big cat is a fierce predator. It can sprint toward prey at up to 37 miles (60 kilometers) per hour. It kills with its sharp claws and crushing jaws. But even this skilled hunter relies on camouflage.

A leopard's spots are brown with black outlines. How do spots help the leopard?

Believe it or not, a leopard's spots help it hide from prey. They form a random pattern on the leopard's body. The pattern breaks up the leopard's shape and the outline of its body. The spots can make it hard to tell where the leopard begins and ends or even that it's an animal at all. The stripes of a tiger or zebra do the same thing.

A leopard's spots help it hide from a zebra. And a zebra's stripes help it hide from the leopard.

A leopard's spots confuse the eye. They make it hard for prey to see the leopard right away. That's especially true when the leopard crouches low and moves slowly. Then *bam!* It pounces on its surprised prey.

A leopard's spots help it blend in too. Leopards often search for prey while hiding in a tree. Their spots match the dark leaves around them. The spots also blend in with the shadows on the ground.

Leopards live in many kinds of habitats. They can be found in grasslands, forests, deserts, and mountains.

Compare It!

Some butterfly fish also have camouflage that confuses predators. These fish have a thin stripe that covers and hides each eye. They also have a black spot that looks like a big eye. When a predator comes close, butterfly fish don't race away. They turn sideways to show their fake eye. The fake eye confuses the predator. If the predator decides to attack, it will try to attack the fish's fake eye. So the fish gets attacked in a less dangerous place.

The butterfly fish's fake eye also might fool a predator into thinking the fish is much bigger than it really is.

Hiding in Plain Sight

You've learned about some amazing ways that animals use camouflage. They can look like objects in nature, such as sticks or leaves. They can disappear into the background by matching the color of their surroundings. They can change colors to match the seasons or change disguises throughout the day. They can even confuse other animals with their spots and stripes. How else do you think animals might hide themselves?

CAN YOU SPOT THE CAMOUFLAGED ANIMAL?

Extinct Animal Superpowers

- The quagga was a mammal that looked like a cross between a zebra and a horse. It had black stripes on its head, neck, and back. The rest of its body was a dark tan. This mix of coloring let it both blend in and confuse its predators.

- The great auk was a flightless bird that spent much of its life in the ocean. It had black feathers on its head and back. The feathers on its underside were white. From above, the bird's dark feathers helped it blend in with the dark sea. From below, its white feathers helped it blend in with the sunlight and sky overhead.

- The giant *Titanoboa* died out nearly sixty million years ago. Its length of 45 feet (14 meters) made it the largest known snake ever to live on Earth. How could such a huge predator sneak up on prey? Its scaly skin probably matched the ground it slithered on.

Glossary

amphibian: a kind of animal that can live in water and on land, such as a frog

habitat: the place in nature where an animal lives

larva: a young insect that has no wings and looks like a worm

mating: getting together to produce babies

predator: an animal that hunts and eats other animals

prey: an animal that is hunted and eaten by other animals

texture: the way something feels when touched, such as smooth, rough, or bumpy

toxic: poisonous. Something that's toxic can kill an animal or make it sick.

tundra: a cold, harsh area of flat land without trees where the soil beneath the ground stays frozen all year

venom: a kind of poison made by certain animals, such as snakes and spiders

Learn More about Animal Camouflage

Books

Franchino, Vicky. *Animal Camouflage*. New York: Children's Press, 2016. Check out this book to discover more fascinating facts about how animals stay out of sight.

Harrison, David L. *Now You See Them, Now You Don't: Poems about Creatures That Hide*. Watertown, MA: Charlesbridge, 2016. Learn about camouflaged creatures through the language of poetry.

Johnson, Rebecca L. *Masters of Disguise: Amazing Animal Tricksters*. Minneapolis: Millbrook Press, 2016. Meet more animals that are amazingly good at fooling predators and prey.

Websites

ARKive
http://www.arkive.org
This site, from the wildlife group Wildscreen, features photos, videos, and audio clips of many animals with information about how they survive.

California Academy of Sciences: Mimic Octopus
https://www.calacademy.org/explore-science/mimic-octopus
Watch this video to see a mimic octopus in action and learn more about this amazing master of disguise.

Pygmy Sea Horses: Masters of Camouflage
http://ww2.kqed.org/science/2014/10/21/pygmy-seahorses-masters
-of-camouflage
Watch this video to see what baby pygmy sea horses look like when they're born and how they change to match their coral home.

Index

Photo Acknowledgments

The images in this book are used with the permission of: © Incredible Arctic/Shutterstock.com, p. 4; © blickwinkel/Alamy, p. 5; © Ray Wilson/Alamy, p. 6; © Premaphotos/Minden Pictures, p. 7; © Richard Hutchings/Science Source, p. 8; © Konrad Wothe/Minden Pictures, pp. 9, 33; © Thomas Marent/Minden Pictures, p. 10; © Piotr Naskrecki/Minden Pictures, p. 11; © Brandon Cole Marine Photography/Alamy, p. 12; © Chanwit Polpakdee/Shutterstock.com, p. 13; © Alex Mustard/Minden Pictures, p. 14; © Clay Bolt/Minden Pictures, p. 15; © CyberEak/Shutterstock.com, p. 16; © Mathieu Meur/Stocktrek Images/Alamy, p. 17; © iStockphoto.com/RyersonClark, pp. 18, 20; © iStockphoto.com/Dawn Nichols, p. 19; © iStockphoto.com/martince2, p. 21; © iStockphoto.com/drferry, p. 22; © Mary Ann McDonald/Shutterstock.com, p. 23; © iStockphoto.com/cdascher, p. 24; © Stubblefield Photography/Shutterstock.com, p. 25; © Ethan Daniels/Alamy, p. 26; © David Fleetham/Alamy, p. 27; © Hans Lang/Getty Images, p. 28; © Aquanaut4/Dreamstime.com, p. 29; © Jeff Rotman/Minden Pictures, p. 30; © Karl Keller/Shutterstock.com, p. 31; © Fritz Polking/Minden Pictures, p. 32; © iStockphoto.com/herbertlewald, p. 34; © Vladislav Gajic/Shutterstock.com, p. 35; © kaschibo/Shutterstock.com, p. 36.

Front cover: © Kevin Wells Photography/Shutterstock.com.

Main body text set in Adrianna Regular 14/20.
Typeface provided by Chank.